Green Planet
RESCUE

Green Planet
RESCUE

Saving the Earth's Endangered Plants
by Robert R. Halpern

A Cincinnati Zoo Book
FRANKLIN WATTS
New York • Chicago • London • Toronto • Sydney

This book is dedicated to
scientists and researchers,
graduate students and field workers
around the world,
and to the people like you
who support them in their efforts
to save wildlife of every kind.

Photographs copyright © : Cincinnati Zoo: pp. 8, 10, 13 right,
15 bottom right, 19, 23
bottom right, 24 left, 33 left, 34 right (all Ron Austing), 14, 15 bottom left
(both Mike Dulaney), 57 (Stan Rullman);
Center for Plant Conservation/Arnold Arboretum: p. 31;
World Wildlife Fund: pp. 48 (Ken Scriven),
49 right (Peter Jackson); The Nature Conservancy/John Kleber: p. 51;
Center for Reproduction of Endangered
Wildlife/Valerie Pence: pp. 53, 54, 55; Kate Wetzel: p. 58;
All other photographs copyright © Rob Halpern.

Library of Congress Cataloging-in-Publication Data

Halpern, Robert R.
Green planet rescue : saving the earth's endangered plants / by
Robert R. Halpern.
p.   cm.—(A Cincinnati Zoo book)
Includes bibliographical references and index.
Summary: Discusses the importance of plants and what can be done
to protect some kinds of plants that face extinction.
ISBN 0-531-11095-8
1. Endangered plants—Juvenile literature.   2. Plant conservation—
Citizen participation—Juvenile literature.   [1. Rare plants.
2. Plant conservation.]   I. Title. II. Series.
QK86.A1H34   1993
581.5'29—dc20   93-105 CIP AC

Green Planet
RESCUE

Rain forests, such as this one in Costa Rica (top), are being cleared at an alarming rate.
The timber is harvested and the land developed for farming and grazing (below).
Hundreds of plant and animal species face extinction as their habitat disappears.

ENDANGERED
Is a Scary Word

"Endangered" sounds like something scary, and it is. "Danger" is right there in the middle of it. But when the subject is endangered plants, it's hard to see what all the fuss is about. Plants just grow, don't they? Weeds sprout in every open space, so what's the problem? There are always plenty of green things out there—everywhere we look. Why is any one plant **species** all that important?

Plants are not great as pets, but they are our companions on this planet. They are important in our lives and in the lives of every other animal. They produce the basic resources for life on Earth. There may be 380,000 or more different species of plants and we know little about many of them. Some species live in such special and small **habitats** that we haven't even found them yet. Can we afford to find out what life without a particular species would be like?

An endangered species is one with a small population whose survival is threatened. Human populations are growing. New roads, buildings, dams, farms, and grazing areas are spreading over the landscape so that little real wilderness is left anywhere. An endangered species will disappear if these conditions continue. An endangered species needs help. Today 20,000 to 25,000 of the plant species on Earth are endangered, vulnerable, or rare. We may be losing something important without even knowing much about it.

WHY
Do Plants Matter?

A PLANET OF PLANTS

Plants provide the resources that people and animals use to live on Earth. They provide nesting sites for birds, camouflage for cheetahs, aerial highways for tree snakes, and beds for gorillas. Desert animals depend on plants for stored water, beavers build dams with plants, while leaf-cutter ants use them to make compost for their fungus gardens. And people use plants for everything.

Green plants use the sun's energy to convert water and oxygen into sugars and starches. These nutrients are then used by many animals for food. Different animals use different parts of each plant, but all parts seem to be eaten by something: caterpillars and koalas eat leaves; deer and rhinos eat twigs; toucans and orangutans eat fruit; hummingbirds and butterflies drink the flowers' nectar; porcupines and gorillas eat the inner bark; moles and bears eat roots. Many other species, from spiders to lions, eat the animals that eat plants. Directly or indirectly, all life on Earth depends on plants.

Facing page: Plants provide nesting material or sites for birds, gorillas, and squirrels; aerial "highways" for monkeys, leopards, and tree snakes; camouflage for lions and hairy turtles; and basic materials for people.

The nutrients plants produce
are used by caterpillars,
koalas, Thomson's gazelles,
and many other animals.

People and our domesticated cows, lambs, chickens, and pigs use only about 30 of the 380,000 plant species for food. Farmers grow millions of acres of wheat, corn, and rice to provide it. In each crop, all the plants are very similar, so a plant disease can spread quickly through it. The harvest can be lost and a whole community might starve. Farm crops were developed from wild plants through centuries of breeding and selection. A surviving wild species could contain traits that might protect a food crop.

New discoveries still revolutionize agriculture. In 1977, a botany student in Mexico found an unusual grassy plant, a species of wild corn, *Zea diploperennis*, that resists several corn-plant diseases. And unlike farm corn, which is an **annual**—that is, planted each year from seed—this species re-grows every spring. The **perennial** corn can survive cold and damp, and so farmers could grow its descendants in areas they couldn't use before. If these traits can be bred into corn crops without reducing their productivity, the discovery of this single plant species could help reduce world hunger.

Newly discovered wild relatives of corn are being studied to see if they can be used to breed disease-resistant strains.

THE RENEWABLE RESOURCE

Plants collect energy from the sun and release it for people to use as fuel. In many countries firewood is still the most important fuel for heat and for cooking. As populations grow around the world, more wood is cut and entire forests disappear up the chimney. But plants are a renewable resource; they can be replanted if seeds are saved.

Plants also provide wood, which we use to construct buildings, boats, and furniture. Today, many exotic hardwoods like teak are harvested from tropical forests, putting stress on already threatened **ecosystems**. Yet teak, native to Southeast Asia, and other valuable hardwoods, can be produced

Wild mahogany (above) and teak are disappearing from the rain forests due to over-harvesting. Some woods can be harvested in limited quantities; others could be grown on plantations.

on large tree farms where the trees are replanted for future crops. In Java, teak is successfully grown on plantations established almost 120 years ago. Trees are harvested when they are eighty years old and the fields are replanted. But in Thailand, more than 80 percent of the teak exported annually is cut from the forests. If teak plantations were expanded, the forests might be saved and local people would have a valuable income source.

The renewable resources of plants might even help save some endangered animals. Whales were hunted for their oil, now used for heavy machinery. An American desert plant, Jojoba or *Simmondsia chinensis*, has been found with seeds that contain an oil similar to sperm whale oil. Unlike whales, jojoba can be grown and harvested on desert farms.

GREEN MEDICINES

Some plants produce chemicals that help them adapt to the environment and protect them from leaf-eating animals. People in every part of the world have discovered that these chemicals have uses as medicine. They are important economically, too; sales of plant-based medicines are worth about $100 million each year.

Plants make many chemicals in response to losing their leaves to leaf-eating animals like the sloth and the panda. The new leaves taste bad, so fewer are eaten by the next animal.

Aspirin was developed from willow trees, based on a remedy used by the ancient Greeks and some Native American tribes. Animals, such as howler monkeys and elephants, search for certain plants when they are sick. Chimpanzees in Gombe National Park in Tanzania pluck leaves from two species of plants and swallow them without chewing. The leaves contain a red, sulfur-rich oil, thiarurbrine-A, which can kill disease-causing bacteria, fungi, and parasitic worms. Chimps swallow the leaves and their oil is released into the animal's bloodstream during digestion. Thiarurbrine-A may also have value as a cancer-fighting drug for humans.

Chimpanzees and other animals eat certain plants to cure illnesses. One fourth of the prescription drugs used today are derived from plants.

Another plant-produced medicine is vinblastine. It comes from a plant grown in many gardens: Rosy periwinkle or *Catharanthus roseus*, a native of the island of Madagascar, southeast of Africa. The chemicals in the Madagascar periwinkle have helped thousands of people survive leukemia and other diseases.

More than ten thousand kinds of plants grow on Madagascar, and 80 percent of them grow nowhere else. Four-fifths of the native vegetation has been destroyed and many plants are disappearing. Not even one percent of the flowering plants on earth have been tested for medicinal properties. How many more of these threatened plants contain chemicals that might cure diseases?

The rosy periwinkle from Madagascar produces a chemical scientists have used to treat leukemia.

Lemurs and Parson's chameleon are among the many species found only on Madagascar. About 11 million people also live on the island, which is approximately the size of Texas. As the population grows, the forests are cut down at a rate of 2,000–3,000 square kilometers each year.

When the habitat changes slowly, plants and animals can adapt. Amazonia was underwater in prehistoric times, and still floods every year. Trees in the Amazon rain forest can survive annual flooding.

These two Japanese Zelkova trees appear identical until autumn when one drops its leaves before the other. What other genetic differences might they have that we can't see?

WHY
Are Plants Endangered?

IT'S GOOD TO BE DIFFERENT

Survival of the species is the most important goal in nature, but sometimes it's not easy. Since before the days of the dinosaurs, the Earth's climate has undergone slow changes. Regions have grown colder or warmer. Areas under water become dry; dry areas are flooded. Usually, these changes take a very long time. Animal and plant species adapt and survive these slow developments. It is much harder when the changes are sudden.

Plants and animals can adapt to change because the individuals within a population are each a little different genetically. Each cell of every living thing carries genes, chemical blueprints, that control how that cell and that individual will grow and develop. In nature, new generations are usually formed from the meeting of male and female members of a species. The combining of the parents' genes creates a new genetic mix in the offspring.

Genes are really a set of possibilities. When a fruit ripens, many seeds are formed and some survive and grow. The seeds may look alike, but there could be small genetic differences. If the environment changes, these differences might provide a key to survival. One seedling may be genetically programmed to have a thicker waxy coating on its leaf. During rainy years, it can resist leaf fungus diseases. Or maybe one seedling is programmed to have a bigger root system. In droughty years, that plant can better absorb the scarce water. If changed conditions make one trait more useful for survival than another, that trait is passed on to a new generation. The species has been able to adapt to changes because of the **genetic diversity** of its population. If change is rapid, or if there are very few individuals, there may not be enough genetic possibilities to enable the species to survive the new conditions. The species disappears.

Tropical forests are areas of even warmth and sunlight. Rain forests have regular rainfall throughout the year. With these growing conditions, many plant and animal species develop. Climate changes over millions of years increase the **species diversity** as small populations of plants and animals become isolated and must adapt to new conditions.

Unfortunately, these Yagua Indians in Peru are abandoning their use of traditional medicines from rain forest plants. Tribal people living in the forests have learned much about the usefulness of plants, but modern scientists still know very little. The experience of the Yagua and other groups could lead to important new medicines if their secrets are shared in time.

HOW A PLANT FINDS A MATE

Genetic diversity requires the mixing of genes from different individual members of a species. Animals accomplish this using many methods to attract mates. Plants are different. Most are rooted to the ground and cannot move about. They need help when it's time to mate. Some plants use wind to blow pollen from flowers of one individual to flowers of another. This is how plants growing in open grasslands (like the American prairie or the African savannah) and the tallest trees in the rain forests are pollinated. Garden corn and forest birch trees are pollinated this way, too. Where there is little wind, as in a jungle, other methods have developed. An animal **pollinator** carries pollen from plant to plant. Flowers have developed special colors, shapes, and smells to attract pollinators. Butterflies, hummingbirds, Australian honey possums, some tropical bats, and many other animals depend on the nectar and pollen they collect from flowers. Flowers may also provide chemicals that the pollinator uses. They may even serve as a place for the pollinators to meet mates.

The great grasslands of the world support vast herds of grazing animals—like these topi in Africa—and the predators that hunt them. Most grasses are pollinated by the wind.

Animals have many ways to attract mates. A male redwing blackbird perches on a post, singing and flashing red shoulder patches to draw females. Plants must attract their pollinators with flowers.

Flowers deposit pollen on the pollinating animal so that it will be carried along and left on the next flower of the same species the animal visits. Usually the pollinator rubs against the flower's **anthers**, where pollen is made, while collecting nectar, pollen, or chemicals. Pollen sticks to the head or body of the visitor. At the next flower the animal visits, it brushes against the pollen collecting surface, the **stigma**, as it feeds on the flower's nectar. In this way, the stigma collects pollen from the last flower visited rather than from itself. This encourages cross-pollination, increasing genetic diversity.

Colorful or fragrant flowers attract pollinating animals. Stapelia gigantea *(left) attracts flies for pollination.* Syzygium malacensis *(right) is pollinated by birds.*

The stigma, *which receives pollen, is raised up in the center of this flower, surrounded by the* anthers, *which produce pollen. Insects visiting this cactus flower brush against the stigma before they can get to the nectar and the anthers.*

How does a plant get the pollinator to deliver its pollen to the **pistil** of another flower of the same species? Pollen from one species will not fertilize the **ovary** of an unrelated species. Some species bloom all at once over a large area, at a time when few other plants flower. They attract many different pollinators and chances are the next flower visited will be of the same species.

Look at goldenrod blooming in the fields in late summer. You will find bees, wasps, butterflies, and beetles crawling over the blossoms. Any one of them can pollinate goldenrod.

In desert habitats, almost all species flower at the same time, after the spring rains. In tropical rain forests, there is no spring or winter, and many types of plants flower every day. Pollinators searching for nectar or pollen could visit dozens of species. Therefore, each kind of plant must attract a pollinator that will specialize in that plant.

Plants must also protect their nectar from animals who might steal it without pollinating the flower. It takes a lot of energy to make nectar to pay a pollinator, but insects and animals don't care whose nectar they eat. Flowers may use colors that only the right pollinator can see. They may have heavy "doors" that only the perfect pollinator can open. They may surround their flowers with water moats to keep away crawling insects. They may bloom only at night when fewer pollinating species are active.

In rain forests, Couroupita guianensis (left) and Clerodendron paniculatum (right) and many other flowers bloom every day. Each must attract a specific pollinator to make sure it receives pollen from another flower of the same species.

BEYOND THE BIRDS AND THE BEES

Bees are the best-known pollinators. Not all bees are alike. Only large bumblebees are strong enough to force their way into a snapdragon flower. Only certain tropical bees have tongues long enough to reach the nectar deep inside a golden allamanda flower.

Many other insects act as pollinators, too. Butterflies are attracted to small tube-shaped flowers that offer a flat landing spot and grow in sunny areas. The butterflies cannot see small flowers from far away, so plants that want to attract them cluster many blossoms together. Each flower in the group reaches peak bloom (that's when the pollen is ripe and there is the most nectar) on a different day, increasing the chances of the plant being pollinated.

Flowers may hide their nectar at the end of tubes that only the right pollinator can reach. A large bee with a long tongue is needed to gather the nectar at the base of this allamanda flower in South America.

*On some plants, like **Lantana camara**, the flowers show the butterfly which are ready by changing their color as they pass their peak. The "over-the-hill" flowers can still guide the butterfly to the plant. Lantana blooms look like a mix of tiny yellow, orange, and red flowers.*

Some bees feed on pollen as well as on nectar. You can see a bee's golden pollen sacs on its rear legs.

In the tropics, hummingbirds and sunbirds transfer pollen, too. Birds are drawn to the color red, and many plants have developed red flowers to attract them. Flowers that depend on hummingbirds must accommodate the hummingbird's behavior. Hummingbirds are very territorial. They visit all parts of their territory throughout the day and defend it from other hummingbirds. Many hummingbird-pollinated plants surround their flowers with red, long-lasting specialized leaves, or **bracts**. Each day one or two small flowers open; the next day new buds replace them. The red bracts remain for weeks or months, attracting the hummingbirds to a succession of small flowers. Hummingbirds require large amounts of nectar for energy. They have long beaks and even longer tongues, so flowers that depend on them protect their abundant nectar from other animals by locating it at the bottom of very long tubes.

Hummingbirds hover in midair as they feed, so they are attracted to flowers that hang down like this Heliconia *(right) or face outward, offering them a clear space. Hummingbirds require large amounts of nectar, which the flowers must protect from theft by ants, bees, and crawling insects.* Heliconia *flowers may be surrounded by a water moat or a sticky goo to keep out anything other than a hummingbird.*

Orchids have strange pollination strategies. One species in Central and South America provides male bees with a chemical they need to attract females. The male bees have brushes on their front legs to collect the oily chemical from the flower. They store it in pouches on their hind legs. Later, they release this chemical when they look for females. Other orchid flowers have evolved so that they actually look like female bees, luring males to come to "mate" with them. Pollen is transferred during these bee activities. Some orchids produce just the smell of nectar, without really having any.

Skunk cabbage blooms in late winter, even pushing up through the snow. This northern relative of tropical philodendrons produces heat chemically. It actually melts snow. When beetles come out to look for mates in winter, they are attracted to the skunk cabbage's warmth. The insects meet and mate on the flower, transferring the plant's pollen at the same time.

Around the world, plants use birds, beetles, wasps, gnats, flies and other insects, bats, and even small mammals as pollinators. Flowers produce whatever it takes to attract their pollinator.

Orchids often trick bees into delivering pollen without providing them with any nectar.
But after visiting a few flowers, the bees seem to catch on and seek other kinds of flowers.
However, once an orchid is pollinated it produces thousands of seeds, so one success is all it needs.

DEPENDING ON EACH OTHER

As flowers evolve to attract particular pollinators, and pollinators evolve to match the flowers, a mutual dependence between plant and animal develops. Each flower's shape gives a clue to the identity of the pollinator. Charles Darwin, a British biologist who lived a hundred years ago, studied an unusual orchid from the island of Madagascar. Nectar was located at the end of a foot-long tube and in the evening the flower produced a strong, sweet fragrance. Darwin guessed that there was a night-flying moth that would be attracted by the smell and would have a proboscis, or snout, that could extend the twelve inches to the bottom of the nectar tube. No one had seen such a moth, and Darwin was not believed. Forty-one years later the moth was discovered. In 1991, scientists studying another species of Mad-

Bat-pollinated flowers open at night
and produce great quantities of nectar.
They may be white, greenish, or purple
and have a strong smell so that night-flying
bats can find them.
These flowers often form on the trunks of the tree,
as does the calabash flower (left),
or hang below the leaves (right), as
on the African sausage tree, allowing
the bats easy access.

agascar orchid with an even longer nectar tube began searching for another undiscovered moth pollinator.

Depending on each other works well for plants and their pollinators. But if one partner gets into trouble, the other is affected. Chocolate comes from the fruit of one species of cocoa plant, *Theobroma cacao*. Its small flowers are pollinated by tiny insects called midges. When cocoa is grown in large tree plantations cleared of other vegetation, fewer fruits form. The reason was discovered centuries ago by the ancient Mayans who found that the midges prefer shade to sunlight and thrive in the leaf litter on the forest floor.

Cocoa trees today are threatened by a fungal disease called moniliphthora. A wild species of *Theobroma* that grows in the Amazon rain forest may be resistant to the fungus, but these wild relatives of the chocolate tree are disappearing as areas of Amazonia are destroyed.

Chocolate comes from the seeds of the cacao tree. The tiny flowers and large fruit form right on the tree trunk and major branches of the tree.

The unusual flowers of Herrania nitida (*above*) *and its close relative,* Theobroma *or cacao, appear directly on the trunk of the tree. These trees are threatened by deforestation in the Amazon region.*

Just as many plants need a particular animal pollinator to help them form seeds to produce a new generation, some animals need certain plants. In the deserts of northern Mexico, century plants, or agave, grow. The name is an exaggeration, but many agave do not bloom until they are thirty years old. Then they send up a 15-foot stalk and burst into magnificent bloom. By day, these flowers provide nectar for bees, moths, and hummingbirds. At night a species of long-nosed bat visits, attracted by a heavy smell the plants produce. The bats are so important for its pollination that the century plant produces chemicals it doesn't use, but that bats need in their diet. The bats cannot survive without the flowers of the century plants, and the flowers cannot be pollinated without the long-nosed bats. But the century plant is under attack. Cattle and deer find the flower stalks delicious and graze on them. Other agave plants are harvested before they flower to make a liquor called tequila. As agave flowers disappear, the bats

Century plants have thick leaves to store water in the dry Mexican desert. Their flowers are a source of nectar for hummingbirds, moths, and bats.

are threatened. Long-nosed bat populations in northern Mexico and south-western United States have fallen so low that the animal is on the endangered list, along with some species of the century plant.

On the tiny island of Mauritius, off the southeast coast of Africa, *Crinum mauritianum* lives today in only one small area. As in nearby Madagascar, native plants are being destroyed as land is turned into farms and pastures. Only about 100 individuals of this plant have been found, growing in a wet area on the edge of a reservoir. Fortunately, the reservoir leaks and cannot be filled to capacity; otherwise, the last remaining crinums would disappear under water. No one knows what insect pollinates the flowers, but because the flowers open just before dark, it may be night-flying hawk moths. If the crinums become extinct, what would happen to this rare insect that scientists have not yet found? What other animals and plants might be affected?

Crinums, which grow in Asia, the Americas, and Africa, have beautiful flowers that attract moths and butterflies.

SAFETY IN NUMBERS

In a number of plant species, some plants are "male" while others are "female." In these **dioecious** species, each plant has either flowers with pollen-producing anthers and no pistil, or flowers with a pistil and no anthers. This plan guarantees cross-pollination since no plant can pollinate itself. However, when the population falls and the few individuals are spread far apart, it may mean that no plant gets pollinated at all.

The islands of Hawaii have some of the most threatened native vegetation in the world. Most of the native plants grow nowhere else. The islands were colonized by Polynesians who brought in animals and plants from their island homes. Sailors from Europe and the United States also brought in plants and animals. These introduced species have done well in Hawaii, but at great cost. Alien plants crowd out the native plants, alien animals eat or destroy the habitat of native plants, and alien animals destroy native animals.

Left: The maidenhair tree, Ginkgo biloba, grew 125 million years ago, when dinosaurs lived. Western scientists had seen only fossil leaves until the tree was found growing in a garden in Japan in 1690. Each ginkgo tree produces either male or female flowers. Once pollinated, the female flowers form small, foul-smelling fruit.

Right: The red fruit of the American holly is produced on plants with female flowers, but they must receive pollen from hollies with male flowers.

The large *Neowawraea phyllanthoides* trees were common on several of the islands of Hawaii. But grazing by introduced cattle and goats, and rooting up by introduced pigs, have destroyed most of the trees. *Neowawraea* is a dioecious plant. Now there are so few left, and these are so widely separated, that pollination is unlikely. The remaining specimens are weak. Unless both male-flowering and female-flowering specimens can be saved, this great tree will disappear.

Even a **monoecious** species, with flowers that have both anthers and pistils, may become endangered if the population becomes too small. Georgia plume, *Elliotia racemosa*, is a large shrub or small tree that grows in small groups scattered through Georgia. It once grew in South Carolina, too, but is now extinct in that state. In early summer, this relative of rhododendrons and azaleas is covered with fragrant, white, star-shaped flowers. Although each Georgia plume has both male and female flower parts, the plants in each location seem to be genetically identical individuals that are unable to cross-pollinate within their group. Pollen from another group is needed. As forests have been cut down, the few remain-

The beautiful Georgia plume may be the rarest American tree. It rarely forms seeds, even in the wild. The first ripe fruit of the plant was not seen until 130 years after the species was discovered.

31

ing populations have become widely separated, making it difficult to produce fertile seed. Luckily, the Georgia Department of Natural Resources has acquired one area where this endangered plant grows and The Nature Conservancy is protecting another. It is hard to grow the plants from seed, but they can be grown from root cuttings and are doing well in several botanical gardens, where plants are grown and studied for scientific and educational purposes, and for their beauty.

Botanical gardens and arboretums (living collections of trees and shrubs) have long been important in saving plants from extinction. In 1765, John and William Bartram, father and son botanists from Pennsylvania, were riding through Georgia looking for interesting plants. Along the banks of the Alatamaha River, they discovered an unusual small tree with large, fragrant white flowers with golden anthers. The Bartrams returned years later, in winter; collected seeds and began growing the plant in their botanical garden in Philadelphia. The tree was named *Franklinia alatamaha* to honor Bartram's friend Benjamin Franklin and its riverbank home. Other botanists saw the trees at the river during the next thirty years. But the Franklin tree has not been seen growing in the wild for about 200 years. What became of this botanical rarity? No one knows for sure. But because of the seeds William Bartram collected, the beautiful Franklin tree, though extinct in the wild, graces many botanical gardens and private landscapes today.

The flowers of Franklinia alatamaha *look like simple camellias, and this American tree is related to those Asian shrubs. The Franklin tree is extinct in the wild.*

ANIMAL GARDENERS

Once seeds are formed they must be planted where conditions are right for growth. If a plant simply drops its seeds on the ground, the seedlings have to compete with the parent plant for light, water, and nutrients. Somehow the seeds must get dispersed, or carried to a new spot.

Although most plants cannot move, many seeds can, or at least they can hitchhike. Dandelion seeds blow away on the wind. Maple seeds fly like helicopters. Coconuts float on rivers and the ocean, eventually landing on a beach. Some seeds hitch rides on you or your pets. Have you ever walked in a field in late summer and found burrs on your clothes or in your dog's fur? These are hitchhiking seeds.

Some plants shoot their seeds to a new spot. Impatiens, a garden flower, produces small round green fruit. When ripe, the slightest touch makes them split apart and the seeds inside shoot out in all directions. A plant related to garden peas shoots its seeds when the sun dries the fruit and it splits.

Many plants use animals to spread their seed. If you spit out watermelon seeds and later see young watermelon plants grow, you are an animal seed disperser. All fruits begin as payments to animals for spreading seeds.

Above: Plants produce many different kinds of fruits and seeds in order to colonize new areas. The seeds may be designed to blow in the wind, or float, or stick to an animal's fur. Seed coats protect the seed from sprouting before growing conditions are right.

Left: What better way to get seeds to a new home than by encouraging a fruit bat to fly off with them and drop them somewhere else? Or getting howler monkeys to drop them from the trees? Or getting chipmunks to plant them in the forest?

Most plants grow only in certain spots or under certain conditions. Mistletoe, a plant found in North and South America, is a parasite—it grows on a host plant, on which it depends for its nutrients and water. How do mistletoe seeds land on the branches of host trees? Why don't they fall to the ground? Mistletoe seeds are coated with a sticky, indigestible substance. In the American tropics, colorful birds called euphonias feed on mistletoe berries. The pulp is digested but the seeds pass through the birds and end up, still with their sticky coating, in the birds' droppings. The birds deliver the seeds to the treetops, and the sticky coating holds the seeds on the branches until they establish roots.

Seeds have a coat that prevents damage and keeps in moisture. Many plant species cannot germinate, or begin to grow, until an animal has digested the seed and weakened the seed coat. On the hot African plains, thorny acacia trees are about the only trees that provide shade. If acacia seeds fall from the tree and germinate where they land, they would lose the competition for water with the parent tree. If the seeds blow away, they might land on poor soil. The acacia fruit looks like a big, dry string bean with a hard shell. Passing giraffes eat the fruit and the protective seed coat is broken down in their cow-like stomachs. The seed passes through the giraffe and is deposited—covered with moist, nutrient-rich giraffe manure, the perfect material for germination. Without the giraffe, the thorny acacia could not reproduce.

Above: Euphonias deposit mistletoe seeds on treetop branches where they can grow.

Right: Acacia trees growing on the hot African savannah are planted by giraffes who eat the fruit and deposit the seed.

What happens if one member of a plant–animal partnership disappears? Another endangered plant from Mauritius is the long-lived Calvaria tree. Scientists have found that all the specimens on the island are at least 300 years old. Why have no seedlings of this tree grown up in the past three centuries? In fact, why has no one ever seen a Calvaria seedling? Scientists tried to get the seeds to germinate, but could not. The seeds are very large and the scientists guessed that there must have been a large bird capable of swallowing the fruit whole. The seed coat would have been weakened during digestion. As an experiment, the scientists fed the fruit to a large bird, a turkey. Seeds collected from the turkey manure did germinate—the first Calvaria seeds to do so in 300 years. Until about 300 years ago, a large bird called the great dodo lived on Mauritius Island. Sailors hunted this seed-disperser to extinction in the seventeenth century, and the trees that depended upon it became endangered. Through research and conservation efforts, the Calvaria may now be saved. But without its natural seed-disperser, it can never again survive on its own.

The calabash tree of Central and South America produces large fruits that local people hollow out to make bowls and other utensils. In the forest the seeds are collected by large rodents called agoutis, that seem to be the only animals capable of chewing through the thick fruit. If agoutis disappeared, what would become of the calabash?

EATEN TO EXTINCTION

While some plants are threatened by natural changes in the environment, the sad truth is that most endangered species are in trouble because of the actions of people like us trying to make better lives for ourselves and our children.

The Byfield fern, *Bowenia serrulata*, isn't really a fern. It is a cycad, a member of a plant family that was common on Earth 190 million years ago. Cycads are tough, attractive garden or house plants that look like palm trees or large ferns. Their leaves are poisonous. The ancient Byfield fern grows in eucalyptus forests and on coastal foothills in Australia. Cattle now graze in these areas, and ranchers, worried about their livestock, destroy the Byfield fern whenever they find it. The leaves of *Bowenia* are also collected for the florist trade. The plant that survived millions of years is today in danger of extinction. Fortunately, it is protected in the Byfield State Forest and in a national park in Australia.

Above: The introduction of non-native livestock animals such as cattle, sheep, and goats, and the use of fragile areas for grazing have placed many plants in jeopardy. Naturalization, or the introduction into the wild of alien animals (like pigs for later hunting), or the escape of domesticated animals (such as rabbits) that adapt too successfully to new environments, have threatened many plants and animals around the world.

Right: The Byfield fern is endangered because of harvesting for the florist trade and because cattle ranchers destroy it to protect their stock from its poisonous leaves.

Buttercups, members of the genus *Ranunculus*, grow in Europe, Asia, and North America. In New Zealand some native buttercups are threatened with extinction. *Ranunculus crithmifolius* ssp. *paucifolius* grows in only one location, at the base of limestone cliffs on South Island. Rabbits, introduced to New Zealand for food during the nineteenth century, like the little buttercup. So do sheep brought to graze in the area. In 1948 there were only thirty-two individuals of the species left. Six years later, the spot was made a reserve and fenced off to protect the plants. The fences are checked regularly, non-native weeds are removed, and *Ranunculus* seeds are collected and planted. With this careful management, the population grew to several hundred plants in less than twenty years.

The future of another important plant is not so bright. Olive trees have been cultivated in the Middle East for thousands of years. Olives are grown from one species of the genus *Olea* (although other related species exist). *Olea laperrinei*, a wild relative, grows in the mountains of the Sahara in northern Africa. The small trees grow very slowly and some are 2,000 to 3,000 years old. In Algeria the Tuareg people cut the branches to feed their

Cycads, like the Byfield fern and this Dioon edule *from Central America, have separate male-flowering and female-flowering plants. Some specimens of* Dioon edule *may be 2,000 years old. Although they evolved before such cone-bearing plants as pine trees, cycads all over the world are endangered today.*

cattle. Since the 1970s, this land (also known as the Sahel) has suffered a terrible drought caused, in part, by overgrazing. In dry regions, when plants that hold the soil and recycle soil moisture to the atmosphere are destroyed, topsoil blows away and rainfall decreases. Deserts expand. In an effort to survive the drought in the Sahel, the people search out every last branch to feed their flocks, placing terrible pressures on the precious native plants. Right now, nothing is being done to save this plant.

PEOPLE CAN BE DANGEROUS

When the needs of people and the needs of plants conflict, plants usually lose. Among the great achievements of the ancient Egyptian civilization was the development of written language and paper. Paper was made from the fibers of the papyrus plant, *Cyperus papyrus*, that grew in the marshes of the Nile delta. But as the Egyptian population increased, river water was diverted for irrigation and marshes were drained for new fields. By the 1830s papyrus was thought to be extinct in Egypt. Then, in 1968 the Egyptian subspecies of papyrus, *Cyperus papyrus* ssp. *hadidii*, was discovered in a few scattered marshes. Now even these remnant sites are drying up and the plant that helped build a great civilization is endangered.

Papyrus (at left), which grows in the marshes of the Nile River area, was used by ancient Egyptians to make paper. Today, draining of the marshes for agriculture has endangered this important plant.

Development of wild lands for farming, housing, and industry creates dangers for many plants. In the United States, Europe, Asia, and Africa, plant species become endangered or even extinct as habitats are torn apart. The coontie-palm, *Zamia floridana*, of Florida and Georgia is, like Australia's Byfield fern, a remnant cycad from prehistoric times. People once made flour from the underground stems of this species. In the early 1900s *Zamia* was so abundant that maps labeled the Florida Keys "Coontie Grounds." All that is changed now; thousands of acres of coastline were bulldozed for homes and resorts. The coontie-palm is not protected in the wild, although it is grown in gardens throughout Florida and southern Georgia.

Using the resources of the land may also threaten plants. Early settlers in Tennessee, Alabama, and North Carolina found a tree with clusters of fragrant white flowers and beautiful wood growing among the native oaks, hemlocks, and hickories. The American yellowwood, *Cladrastis lutea*, ranges into Ohio, Indiana, Missouri, and Oklahoma. This rare tree has been around for 50 million years, but is now another vulnerable species. Its woodland home is being flooded by dams or cleared. Because it tends to

The American yellowwood (above) has beautiful white flowers in spring. Early settlers used the close-grained wood to make rifle stocks, and the roots produced a clear yellow dye for fabrics.

The coontie-palm (right) has been around for millions of years, but is endangered today in its native Florida as land is cleared for development.

have a split or double trunk, forest managers remove it to encourage more commercially valuable species. Like the coontie-palm, the American yellowwood is a beautiful landscape plant and is grown in botanical gardens and occasionally in nurseries. Some wild stands are protected in the Great Smokey Mountains National Park, but other populations are poorly protected.

The Great Smokey Mountains contain a wealth of plant species. Many are preserved in the Great Smokey Mountains National Park.

STEALING FOR THE GARDEN

Plant-lovers often want to see their favorites in their gardens or indoor collections. Where do we get these plants? Most are grown from seeds or cuttings in nurseries. Tulip bulbs are shipped from Holland; tropical plants are grown in Central America. Cut flowers for florists come from Israel, Ecuador, Hong Kong, and elsewhere. These businesses are important to the nations' economies.

Plants are also collected in their native habitats for sale to gardeners. Bulbs, including tulips and daffodils, are actually a plant species' special adaptation to harsh seasonal growing conditions. Most come from gravelly hills where a long moist spring is followed by a longer hot and droughty summer. The plants must grow, flower, and set seed quickly, and then go dormant during the summer. They store nutrients and water in specialized leaves, stems, or roots. When rains and warmth return, the yearly cycle begins again.

Plants grown in nurseries, such as these tropical Dracaenas, *or corn plants, in Costa Rica, make the best garden or house plants. Do not buy plants collected from the wild.*

Many garden bulbs come from Turkey and western Asia, around the Black Sea. Here, entire villages survive by harvesting wild bulbs and selling them to merchants; the bulbs are shipped to Holland and eventually reach your garden. Many of these species are common, and harvesting doesn't threaten their survival. But other species are rare, and may disappear from their native habitats if collecting is not controlled. As long as the species are grown in gardens, they will not actually disappear. But native populations are needed to guard genetic diversity. Conservation groups are studying ways to control trade in wild bulbs, and in 1990 the Dutch bulb industry agreed to restrict the sale of these plants. Fortunately, most daffodils and tulips are garden hybrids, not wild species. They have been developed and produced in gardens.

Some popular spring-flowering bulbs, including snowdrops, Galanthus nivalis *(left), and wild tulips,* Tulipa pulchella *(right), are collected from the wild in Portugal and Turkey.*

Plants that eat animals are especially fascinating and when we see a Venus's-flytrap, *Dionea muscipula*, for sale we may be tempted to buy it. Carnivorous, or flesh-eating, plants have developed mostly in sunny, acidic bogs, where nutrients are scarce. Pitcher plants, or *Nepenthes*, of southeast Asia, sundews or *Drosera* species of southern Africa, South America, and Australia, and many insectivorous (insect-eating) species from the bogs of New Jersey and the Carolinas have their own ways to catch and digest insects. But growing Venus's-flytraps and other carnivorous plants from seed is expensive, so if you see inexpensive plants for sale, they were probably collected in the wild. Thousands are gathered every year in the Carolina bogs. Once sold, most will die. They were not very safe in the bogs, either. The bog habitats of Venus's-flytrap are being drained, filled, and planted with pine trees for the timber industry. Without protection, this unique plant soon will be endangered.

Carnivorous or meat-eating plants, like the Venus's-flytrap (left), are collected from the bogs of New Jersey and the Carolinas. They usually do not survive long as house plants. Pitcher plants, like this Sarracenia purpurea (right), are threatened in some states.

Boggy areas are important for wildlife. As they are drained for development, native plants and animals disappear.

Garden plants are descended from native species from all parts of the world. The daylilies growing at the mailbox came from Asia, and the roses along the fence are from China and Europe. You may have thought these plants were American natives. These species escaped from gardens (thanks to seed dispersers) and are naturalized here.

However, when imported plants make homes for themselves in wild areas, they can threaten native species. Fields and forest edges in our southern states are smothering under kudzu, *Pueraria lobata*, a vine introduced from China and Japan. It was planted here as a food for cattle and to control erosion. But kudzu has grown so abundantly that it has become a pest. Native vegetation in Hawaii is under attack from introduced plants, also. In Australia, American prickly-pear cactus is causing similar problems. Tampering with ecosystems can backfire when not enough is known about how plants will behave in a new environment.

Purple loosestrife, Lythrum salicaria, *was introduced into American gardens from Europe. Its seeds found their way into damp meadows and wetlands where it spread rapidly, overtaking native species. To slow its spread, the sale of purple loosestrife has been declared illegal in several states.*

WHAT
Can You Do?

WHAT'S THE PROBLEM?

How much do we know about life on Earth? How many plant species are there and how do they grow? How are they pollinated, who eats their fruit and disperses their seed, how are they used by other plants and animals? For a huge number of species, we don't know the answers. Thousands of plant species may be as yet undiscovered.

Taking inventory of the world's species is an enormous task. But as human development spreads to new areas, we need to find out quickly just what is out there. Recruiting biologists and botanists, sending them into the field, and analyzing the data they collect is expensive. Governments and universities in many countries have begun this work; they need help and expert advice.

The International Union for the Conservation of Nature and Natural Resources (IUCN) was formed in 1948 by citizens, scientists, and conservation groups to gather information on threatened wildlife, raise awareness of conservation problems, recommend solutions, and give technical support to conservation efforts. To raise money for these programs and spread the word about conservation, the IUCN created the World Wildlife Fund (WWF) in 1961.

Botanists still discover surprising plants when exploring remote areas. The dawn redwood, Metasequoia glyptostroboides, existed 50 million years ago and was thought extinct. In 1941 Chinese botanists rediscovered this living fossil, which bears cones like a pine tree but sheds its leaves in autumn. Today, although it is still rare in the wild, it thrives in gardens, thanks to these botanical pioneers.

World Wildlife Fund works with local groups to develop plans to save wilderness while creating jobs and economic security. Conservation education in classes like this one in Malaysia teach local children the importance of plants. WWF is also involved in legal battles over wildlife conservation issues.

Rain forests around the world are being bulldozed, cut, and burned at an alarming rate. Often areas are destroyed before anyone except local inhabitants knows what is there. Wildlife Conservation International, a branch of NYZS/The Wildlife Conservation Society, has created a Rapid Assessment Program (RAP) to rush teams of biologists in to evaluate threatened areas. The teams, working with local scientists, decide which areas are of greatest value and need protection. Their recommendations are submitted to the government of the host country. Conservation International follows up by fundraising and efforts to influence local governments to preserve these lands.

Commercial use of endangered species puts pressure on plants and animals already in trouble. A 1973 international agreement, the Convention on International Trade in Endangered Species (CITES), limits or prohibits people from importing or exporting endangered species. Species are added to the list (or occasionally removed from it) as their status changes. However, some countries have not joined CITES and many that have joined do

People found smuggling endangered species into a country may be arrested and their plants or animals confiscated. An official (above) examines animal skins smuggled through Hong Kong.

Dr. Alwyn Gentry (left), a botanist working with Conservation International, collects information on threatened plants of the Amazon.

not enforce the agreement. Another problem is that governments disagree on the level of threat, and debate which species to protect while special interest groups lobby to keep species off the protected lists for economic reasons.

These and similar organizations need your help. You can become involved, receive information through newsletters and books, raise money locally to help them, participate in their educational work, and write letters to government leaders.

GUARDING THE PLANTS

Plants and their natural habitats are being saved by citizens in many countries. Privately run biological reserves, like the Monteverde Cloud Forest Reserve in Costa Rica, raise money to buy a specific area and protect it. Monteverde is a joint project of the Tropical Science Center in Costa Rica and the local community. It receives funds from the World Wildlife Fund, The Nature Conservancy, and others. You can support these efforts in other countries, and you can get involved in your own state. In many towns and counties, local groups take responsibility for a small piece of the local ecosystem and set up a nature center, open space, sanctuary, or other arrangement to protect it. Your help is needed: creating and maintaining trails, raising funds, guiding visitors, removing non-native plants. You can usually find out about local conservation groups through your library or a local nature center.

Many governments have established parks and reserves where it is illegal to damage or remove plants. Reserves such as the Monteverde Cloud Forest in Costa Rica have been created by local citizens to save habitats. Scientists and students may study the area, and tourists may visit to enjoy and learn about the ecosystem, its plants, and its animals.

The Nature Conservancy buys tracts of land in the United States and Latin America to protect their biodiversity, managing the reserves themselves or transferring them to government conservation agencies. It has protected over 5 million acres since its first project in 1954. Recognizing that the involvement of local citizens is essential in any conservation effort, The Nature Conservancy's International Program works through local chapters in the United States and with local conservation organizations in Central and South America. One current project is the Sian Ka'an Reserve on the Caribbean coast of the Yucatan Peninsula, Mexico. The Conservancy and a local group are working with fishermen and Mayan people to make sure that their ways of life are respected in a management plan for the new park. Without strong local support, no park or reserve can succeed.

The Nature Conservancy protects and restores important wild areas throughout North and South America. Tree-planting projects expand habitats for plants and animals.

PLANT RESCUES

The best safeguards of genetic diversity are protected reserves of plants in their natural ecosystems. But if a species is protected in only one reserve, it is vulnerable to natural disasters such as hurricanes or floods, or to vandalism or accidents. As insurance, botanists grow endangered plants in botanical gardens. This is often complicated because the plants need the right soil types, temperatures, amounts of water, and seasonal changes to simulate what happens in nature. And a large, diverse population must be maintained to guarantee genetic diversity.

A botanical garden is a living museum that collects plants and displays and studies them. The Center for Plant Conservation (CPC), founded in

Botanical gardens in every country collect, preserve, and display plants for study and recreation.

1984, coordinates the work of all botanical gardens in the United States to save endangered American species. The CPC organizes efforts to safeguard plants, targets specific species, and eliminates duplication among gardens. The CPC, located at the Missouri Botanical Garden in St. Louis, also works with the United States Department of Agriculture to develop a seed storage program for rare American plants. Botanical gardens work together internationally, too, under the leadership of the IUCN.

At the Cincinnati Zoo and Botanical Garden in Ohio, scientists and volunteers at the Center for Reproduction of Endangered Wildlife (CREW) discover ways to preserve seeds of endangered tropical and temperate plants, as well as techniques for growing rare plants using tissue culture. In this technology, also called cloning, scientists take a small part of a plant and cut it into dozens or even hundreds of cells. Each cell can be grown into a complete plant. The result is large numbers of genetically identical plants. These can be used to meet collectors' demands for rare plants, and

Laboratory-grown Trillium *plants can be sold to gardeners to reduce collecting pressure on the wild populations.*

At the Center for Reproduction of Endangered Wildlife, over-collected species—such as this rare Hexastylus—*are cloned, to produce genetic duplicates.*

reduce pressure on wild populations. Some of the tissue-culture plants could be returned to the wild, but unless they were developed from plants of several populations, they lack genetic diversity. Seeds collected from wild populations and stored in liquid nitrogen at −196°C in "The Frozen Garden" preserve genetic diversity for the future. They can be thawed and germinated when needed to reintroduce plants in the wild. Techniques discovered at CREW will help other botanical gardens and conservation groups save more plants.

Botanical gardens are in every state, and in almost every country. Volunteers help take care of plants and work in labs. Many gardens offer classes and summer programs for students. By studying botany and related subjects, students may prepare for careers working with endangered plants in universities and botanical gardens.

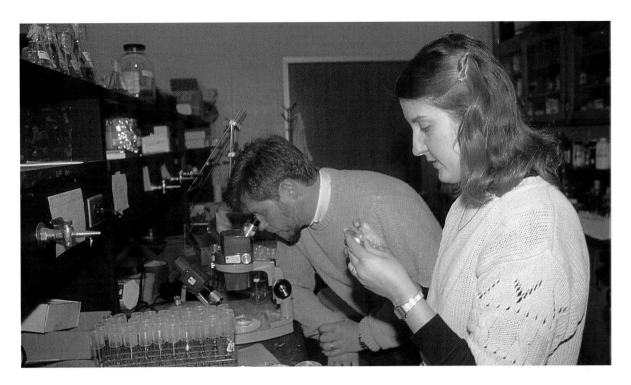

Scientists at the Cincinnati Zoo and Botanical Garden are working to discover ways to preserve seeds of endangered species.

JOIN THE CLUB

People like you can help to protect plants by learning about endangered species, and spreading the word of their importance and the need to stop their destruction. People working together can do amazing things.

The trees of northern India have been cut down as lumber and to fill local villagers' need for firewood. Without the forest, the slopes of the Himalayas are eroding. Villages below are suffering frequent floods and landslides. When the government gave permission for some of the last trees to be cut to make tennis racquets, neighbors objected and organized to save the trees. Village people went into the forest to stop the loggers, hugging the trees so that they could not be cut. The loggers left, the government changed its policy, the trees were saved, and a new conservation group, the Chipko Andolan, was created in India. (The word Chipko means "hugging the trees.")

Twelve-year-old Andrew Holleman learned, in 1987, that a wetland near his Massachusetts town was to be drained so homes could be built. The 17-acre site was home to wild orchids, red fox, and other species. Andrew organized the people of the community to oppose the destruction. They raised funds and petitioned the local zoning board to refuse the building permit. The homes were not built and now Andrew is raising money so the town can buy and preserve the area. Andrew Holleman became the youngest person to receive the United Nations Environment Programme (UNEP) Global 500 Award for outstanding environmental achievement.

Deforestation leaves the soil exposed to erosion. Tree leaves shade the ground from the sun and shelter it from wind and rain, which would remove nutrients. Roots hold fragile soils so they don't get washed away. Erosion removes the fertile topsoil needed for plant growth, causes landslides, or clogs streams and rivers.

Most communities have conservation groups working to save plants. Even in New York City, the Audubon Society preserves wetlands for plants and birds. In Nebraska, the state arboretum maintains prairie restorations around the state. In Dayton, Ohio, a wildflower society distributed petitions to save a local wildlife area and protect an endangered daisy. In every community, Scouts, 4-H Clubs, nature centers, friends of local parks, and other groups are helping preserve plants. Find out what is going on around you and get involved. Check your library for information on local and national conservation organizations. If your town doesn't have a group, contact the state or national office of The Nature Conservancy, Sierra Club, National Wildlife Federation, Audubon Society, or other conservation group to learn how you can start a chapter. You and your classmates can start an ecology club at school. Find out where wildlife is in trouble in your community or state and see what you can do. Everyone's help is important.

Students study the effects of acid rain on bogs in Canada.

*Scouts and other groups participate in many conservation projects
including rescuing wildflowers, cleaning up parks, and maintaining nature trails.*

SAVING
Endangered Plants

Do plants matter? They are important to the life of this planet. Do plants really matter? They are essential to the existence of hundreds of thousands of species of animals from ants to tigers. Are we sure that *all* plants matter? Medicines, foods, and other products we derive from plants make life for all humans possible, and newly discovered plant species provide new medicines and foods to help us survive into the future. Plants are also wonderful miracles of evolution and expressions of life. How can we judge their worth or decide that any species is not important?

There is really only one way to help endangered plants. Get involved. The conditions that threaten plants worsen every day and new plants are added to the endangered species list. To do nothing is to allow the destruction to continue. Your letters to government leaders and corporate executives do affect their decisions. Your petitions, rallies, and fund raising *do* lead to changes for the good.

GLOSSARY

Annual: a plant that grows until it sets seed and dies. The seed germinates, creating the next generation of annual plants.

Anther: the part of a flower that produces pollen.

Bracts: specialized leaves that may resemble flower petals but often last longer. The showy part of a Christmas poinsettia or a dogwood blossom is made up of bracts.

Dioecious: producing female flowers (having a pistil) and male flowers (producing pollen) on separate plants. American hollies are dioecious: the red berries are on plants that have female flowers, but the fruit can not be produced without pollen from a nearby plant with male flowers.

Ecosystem: interrelating plants, animals, and microorganisms and their environment.

Genus (pl. genera): a group of plants (or animals) that are closely related and similar, according to the science of classifying living things by their relationships (called taxonomy). A genus contains one or more species. Related genera are a *family*. It is rare for genera to interbreed. If related plant species within the same genus are interbred, the result is a *hybrid*. The species that produces chocolate is *Theobroma cacao*. *Theobroma* is the genus; *Theobroma cacao* is the species. Another species in the genus *Theobroma* is *Theobroma ovata*.

Habitat: the place where a plant or animal species is usually found.

Hybrid: the result of cross-fertilization or interbreeding of two closely related species.

Monoecious: having pistils and stamens in the same flower.

Ovary: the part of the plant's pistil that forms seeds.

Perennial: a plant that lives longer than one growing season, with a dormant period, or period of no or little growth.

Pistil: the part of a flower that receives pollen; it includes the ovary, which forms seeds.

Pollinator: any animal, including insects and gardeners, that transfers pollen from plant to plant. Pollinators are attracted by colorful flowers, fragrances, ultraviolet markings, or other specific traits.

Seed dispersal: the manner in which a seed gets from the parent plant to the place where it will grow.

Species: a group of plants or animals with common characteristics. A unit of classification within a genus (see **Genus**). Scientists use the classifying term *subspecies* to indicate that there are enough genetic differences to make separate groups within a species. All individuals within a species are potentially able to interbreed.

CONSERVATION ORGANIZATIONS

Center for Plant Conservation
Missouri Botanical Garden
P. O. Box 299
St. Louis, MO 63166

**Center for Reproduction of
Endangered Wildlife**
Cincinnati Zoo & Botanical Garden
3400 Vine St.
Cincinnati, OH 45220

Conservation International
1015 18th St., NW, Suite 1000
Washington, DC 20036

Greenpeace, USA
1436 U St., NW
Washington, DC 20039

League of Conservation Voters
1150 Connecticut Ave., NW
Washington, DC 20036

The National Wildflower Research Center
2600 FM 973 North
Austin, TX 78725

National Wildlife Federation
1400 16th St., NW
Washington, DC 20036

The Nature Conservancy
1815 N. Lynn St.
Arlington, VA 22209

**New England Wildflower Society
Garden in the Woods**
180 Hemenway Rd.
Framingham, MA 01701

Rain Forest Action Network
301 Broadway, Suite A
San Francisco, CA 94133

The Sierra Club
730 Polk St.
San Francisco, CA 94109

Wildlife Preservation Trust International
34th St. & Girard Ave.
Philadelphia, PA 19104

The Wilderness Society
900 17th St., NW
Washington, DC 20036

World Wildlife Fund
1250 24th St., NW
Washington, DC 20037

Wildlife Conservation International
NYZS/The Wildlife Conservation Society
185th St. & Southern Blvd.
Bronx, NY 10460

FOR FURTHER READING

Bernhardt, Peter. *Wily Violets & Underground Orchids: Revelations of a Botanist.* New York: William Morrow & Co., 1989.

Durrell, Lee. *State of the Ark: An Atlas of Conservation in Action.* London: Gaia Books, 1986.

Forsyth, Adrian, and Kenneth Miyata. *Tropical Nature: Life and Death in the Rain Forests of Central and South America.* New York: Charles Scribner's Sons, 1984.

Huxley, Anthony. *Green Inheritance: The World Wildlife Fund Book of Plants.* Garden City, N.Y.: Doubleday/Anchor, 1985.

Meeuse, Bastiaan, and Sean Morris. *The Sex Life of Flowers.* New York: Facts on File, 1984.

INDEX